Are You a "Crazy" Baby Mama?

A Handbook for Single Moms

Max-Laine and Melanie Bent

iUniverse, Inc.
New York   Bloomington

Are You a "Crazy" Baby Mama?
A Handbook for Single Moms

Photography By: Xuchi

iUniverse books may be ordered through booksellers or by contacting:

iUniverse
1663 Liberty Drive
Bloomington, IN 47403
www.iuniverse.com
1-800-Authors (1-800-288-4677)

ISBN: 978-1-4502-3445-0 (sc)
ISBN: 978-1-4502-3447-4 (dj)
ISBN: 978-1-4502-3446-7 (ebook)

Printed in the United States of America

iUniverse rev. date: 07/07/2010

To Our Son, Daughter, & Four-legged Kids

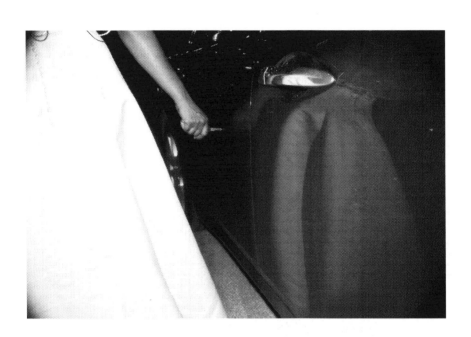

To Whom It May Concern...

It's hard to be biased when trying to encourage other single mothers to better their lives. Especially when we're dealing with drama in the moment of writing this book such as foreclosure, car repossession, our children's fathers, our careers, kids, and financial instability. At first, when we came up with the idea to write this book, our main focus was to make sure that we did not come off as male bashers. Considering this is a sensitive subject where emotions are involved, we are not apologetic when it comes to voicing our opinions and experiences. As mothers, we are sometimes limited to the amount of emotions we can express because we are just that: *mothers*. As single mothers we are EXPECTED to be less emotional and more interactive with our children because of our circumstances. We are exposed to daily criticisms and judgments by family members, friends, co-workers, and anyone who knows that we are single moms. It's no wonder why we're considered "crazy" when we finally do let out our emotions and it's because of all the crap we have to deal with on a daily basis. Once we shared our experiences and other stories of family members and friends experiences as single mothers with each other it was the same story and drama shared among us. For generations, we have made the same mistakes as our mothers, grandmothers, and great-grandmothers have. Isn't it time to let it go and give our children a chance to not make the same mistakes? Sometimes it's just a matter of communicating with our children that will prevent them from making the same mistakes that we made.

The wounds are fresh and this book is our outlet to heal and give us closure. So as we share our story with you, please understand that this book is written by REAL single mothers that have REAL LIFE experiences in dealing with deadbeat fathers while balancing our duties and emotions. There is no type of degree that an individual can earn when it comes to "CRAZY" Baby Mama issues. We like to call it, 'Real Life-ology.' We were tired of listening to contrived information about single mothers from people who had no clue about our daily struggles and frustrations. No one has ever discussed our major issue: raising a child on your own with no physical, emotional, or financial support from the child's father. We want to voice the truth and if we don't accept the truth, then it will be difficult to change our situation. We know firsthand that this statement is true because for a longtime we ignored the signs that our children's fathers showed us at the beginning of the relationship as too many single mothers have. So call us whatever you want. Just know that we are sharing our experiences to start a movement. We are starting a movement for single mothers to reinvent themselves rather than saying that we are starting over. We want to reconstruct the image of a single mother rather than being referred to as a "crazy" baby mama. For so long single mothers have been held accountable by society to raise children; to become productive citizens. But men who abandon their children are not punished, scrutinized, or encouraged more to care for their children.* This movement will push us toward a future where our own children will not have to sacrifice and struggle to raise their children. We must educate and expose the real life of a single mother to encourage deadbeat fathers and potential future deadbeats to help raise the children they created. Some of us who have been raised by single mothers have seen it firsthand as our mothers worked several jobs to support their family where there was no father figure in the home. So why are we facing the same issues our mothers faced? It's time to break the cycle and if you're ready to join this movement read on!

*We understand that there are single fathers who share our same struggles. However, this book is based on our experiences and do not discredit their efforts.

Introduction:

Have you ever wanted to slash your Baby Daddy's car tires? Have you ever wanted to follow him throughout the day to see where he goes? Have you ever wanted to jump on the hood of your Baby Daddy's car after seeing him with his "new girlfriend?" Have you ever wanted to throw his belongings out on the front lawn? Have you ever wanted to make it impossible for him to see his child(ren)? Have you ever wanted to call his job continuously so that it would get him fired? Have you ever wanted to key his car? Have you ever wanted to physically do harm to him after a heated argument? Have you ever wanted to call the police to get him arrested for no particular reason? Have you ever wanted to smash all of his car windows? Have you ever ended the relationship with him only to get back together weeks later?

Well, if you've answered "YES!" to any of these questions, you're probably what some people (maybe your child's father) consider to be a "Crazy" Baby Mama. Please don't get technical on us for using the word 'crazy' because you're probably rolling your eyes and neck saying to yourself "I am NOT crazy." As you can see we placed the word in quotation marks for those of us who don't have a crazy bone in our body. But sometimes the ones who know us the best have a keen sense of knowing how to piss us off and who else can fit that description but a Baby Daddy? When some of us get pushed to the edge we're likely to commit acts that are normally considered *uncharacteristic* of ourselves. We can be perceived as a professional woman one minute and a beast the next minute by slashing all four of his tires in the middle of the night while wearing stilettos.

Once you can get over yourself and admit that if you were pushed (or have experienced being pushed) to the edge, you would more than likely commit these acts – if you haven't done so already or at least contemplated it. The next thing to do is to understand that these feelings are felt among a lot of single mothers toward their child's father across the world no matter what shade of color you are, including us! But if you don't see anything wrong with slashing his car tires, or jumping on the hood of his car, or preventing him from seeing his child (ren), or ANY of the other acts mentioned, then you're probably PSYCHO and we STRONGLY advise that you put this book down and call your local mental health center because we can't help you. We are two single mothers who either had these thoughts or embarrassingly enough have committed one of the above-mentioned acts.

Let's face it, most of us would never have imagined that one day we would end up having ill-feelings towards our child's father. How did it happen? How did we get here? Well hopefully, we can help you deal with those feelings so that you don't internalize it and that you can move forward to living a healthier and better you! As single mothers, we are viewed as strong individuals whose primary job is to raise our children; a job for which we will never receive a paycheck or earn any vacation days. If we had a choice, we wouldn't have to struggle to pay bills and make sure food is on the table without any physical or child support from their father. In fact, we do have a choice to take a stand and to let those deadbeat fathers and possibly future deadbeats know that it's not acceptable for them to neglect their children who didn't have a choice in choosing their parents. We have to accept some responsibility that we put ourselves in this situation and not always point the finger in the other direction. We believe once we do that we can strive to make better decisions for the future. We have to become better examples for our children, so we can't allow them to accept the idea that it's okay for their fathers to walk out of their lives. It's definitely not okay for mothers to degrade their child's father in front of them either. We must teach our sons to be more responsible and teach our daughters to make better decisions than we did. Our minds and bodies take a toll when we birth children and don't have the support from their fathers. So imagine your child growing up to do the same. It would be beneficial for us to give them the tools to be healthy-minded individuals. Let us give them a chance to have a successful life and successful loving relationships and follow this golden rule: *If you fail to plan, then you plan to fail.*

A lot of mothers want to genuinely change their situation but don't know how or don't make the time to figure it out. We want others to resolve our issues or ignore them by jumping into another relationship where we make the same mistakes from previous relationships and are left wondering what went wrong. Did you take time to heal? The healing process may not be an option for a lot of us because we become hopeful women who look for any and all signs for possible changes in our circumstances. One day we're saying that we're going to swear off men and go on a man-fast. Whereas the next day, we may end up at a gas station where we think we've met the man of our dreams because he's driving an expensive car, wearing expensive clothes, says he has no kids, and he can't believe that a pretty young thing like yourself doesn't have a man. Instead of throwing up the peace sign and continuing with your day, you give him your phone number with the <u>expectation</u> (remember this word) that he'll call you later that evening. Then weeks turn into months with no call from your Prince Charming in the shiny new car that was probably worth more than your entire yearly salary. Yet again, you find yourself feeling rejected. There you are sitting on your living room sofa on a Friday night with toys strewn throughout your home, reminded that you still don't have enough money to cover utilities and Johnny needs new shoes with only less than a month left in the school year. We believe the old saying, "Drop that zero and a get yourself a hero." Stop thinking that way. Instead, drop that zero and become YOUR own hero!! Save yourself first because if there were enough heroes to go around there wouldn't be millions of single mothers out there.

Things aren't going to change overnight and you're going to need a lot of patience. It's going to take a huge commitment to make changes in your life. It may be traveling, learning a new hobby, seeking therapy, joining a club with members with similar interests as your own, writing in a journal, or taking a break in dating so that you can know who you really are and what you want in your life. Once we have children we stop taking care of ourselves. Instead, we focus on our children's needs and tend to neglect the things that used to make us happy. We put people and things on the back burner such as our girlfriends, appearance, social life, education, hobbies, dreams, goals, and career. We'll put these things off for a later date and provide excuses which one of many is once your child goes to college that's when you see you'll have the time to pursue those dreams and goals. The most beautiful thing about our lives is that we don't have to wait for anything. As single mothers we juggle so many activities, why can't we include those things that matter to us while raising our kids. If we don't we'll become bitter old women that abandon our true self in order to raise our kids. You don't want to resent your child's success because you never fulfilled your dreams before you got older.

Too many times, single mothers are referred to as baby mamas; to the point that we have songs to encourage us to be strong. That's why we struggled to use the phrase for the title of the book. However, we believe that being a "baby mama" is a state of mind. Like so many other derogatory names we cannot allow those words determine who we truly are. We know that we are committed to our children that we are not going to raise them to become a baby mama or baby daddy, but rather, a responsible and emotionally healthy adult.

The inspiration for this book came about one late night, as we spoke about our financial problems, goals, setbacks, kids and children's fathers; we realized that we both shared the same experiences and feelings towards our children's father but reacted differently when expressing our emotions. We both had a level of expectation from our mates and those expectations grew more after we gave birth to our children. Whether, it was marriage or building a strong bond between our children and their fathers, we want to share those experiences with single mothers across the world in this book. We would rather become the voice for single mothers who struggle each day to provide for their children instead of individuals who are paid to perform statistical reports that don't fully explain why there are so many women becoming single mothers.

Although, we have come a long way from the urge to slash their car tires we believe that sharing our experiences and stories of others will help YOU understand that you're not alone. We have many goals for this book:

1. To educate women and young girls the truth about being a single mother;

2. Expose the deadbeat fathers' tactics;

3. Encourage those fathers who have accepted their responsibilities in caring for their children;

4. Encourage rather than DIScourage men who are not in their child's lives to become active fathers in providing a helping hand in raising their child;

5. To express our emotions, pains, and struggles as a healing and closure process.

Most importantly for single mothers who struggle with their feelings toward their child's father and to inspire the "Crazy Baby Mama" in YOU to find peace in your heart and your relationship with the father of your child(ren).

Ask yourself these questions that we had to ask ourselves: Will I be proud if my daughter becomes a baby mama? Will I be okay if my son grows up to be a deadbeat father? By the end of this book, we hope that you're encouraged to make the necessary changes to continue to provide a better life for your children but most importantly get YOURSELF in a better mind-frame.

When it comes to our children we would give them the world if we could. We work multiple jobs to make ends meet; we make sure our children eat before we eat; we sacrifice our dreams and goals so that our children can have a better life than we did. In return, we neglect ourselves. Is that fair? No, most of those deadbeat fathers end up hurting other woman and getting them pregnant only to leave them with more fatherless children. It will continue to be a cycle and if we're not careful, OUR children and YOURS will become Baby Mamas and Baby Daddies as well.

This is why we wrote this book because we are products of not having fathers in our own lives. Melanie doesn't want her son nor do I want my daughter to go through life feeling neglected and making the same mistakes we made in our relationships. We've learned through sharing our experiences with one another that the mistakes we made in our relationships were not only with our children's fathers but with family members and friends as well. We found that we gravitated to people who contributed nothing more than negativity and havoc in our lives. Writing this book is taking us on a journey to heal together and with you. As you are reading this book we are healing and we hope that our shared experiences will not only enlighten you but encourage you to take a close look at yourself on how you're feelings and actions toward your child's father can severely impact your child's relationship with their father and their entire life.

Max-Laine & Melanie

Velocity

Sitting still with no initiative
Holding onto past dreams, past movements and past wishes
Where has my faith gone?
Do you know where I placed it?
Wait, hold on, just a second…
Can I just get a moment?
You mean you want it right now?
I have no energy
I have no inspiration
I have no motivation to want more
Can I tell you how many times I have made…
Promises, to you, and to you, and you but…
I have yet to come through
Holding onto past dreams, past movements and past wishes
And *change* has past me by
Holding onto twenty extra pounds in my right and left pockets
Where has my faith gone?
Do you know where I placed it?
Wait, hold on, just a second…
Can I get a moment?
You mean right now?
I have no energy
I have no inspiration
I have no motivation to want more
Can I tell you how many times I have made…
Promises, to me, and to me, and to me…
I have yet to come through
Sounds like stagnation
Hold up, stop, give me a minute…
A spark is the only thing needed
To move the crowd
Why don't you move forward?
Grab back those dreams, movements and wishes.
Excuses is the way of defeat
So *you have to become the change* that you saw to move ahead
Hold your head high and straighten out your shoulders
Push that attitude out the door and pull that inspiration in

The time has come for the movement to begin
Embrace your dreams, start your own movement and those wishes will come true
The spark that I ignited has begun to shine through
Velocity is the movement that will begin with you!

~Melanie Bent

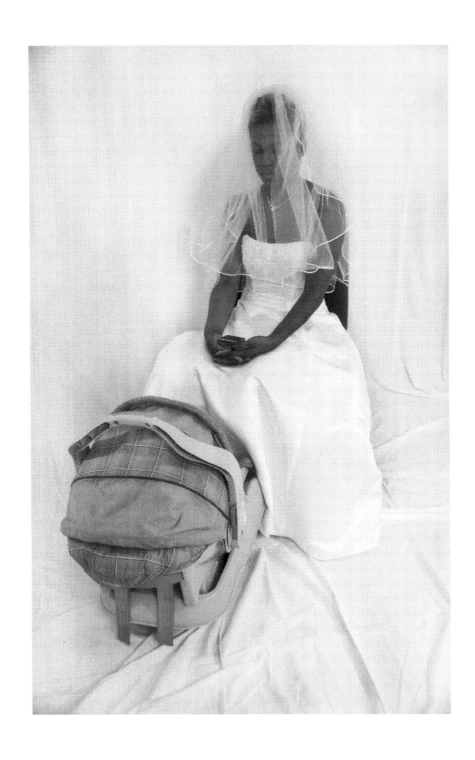

Chapter 1
The "Wedding Dress Theory"

Nowadays, it's unreal to meet couples that are married with children. Our culture has accepted and adopted the notion that once you've entered into a relationship with someone and it results in having a child that there is no obligation to get married. **As of 2009, sixty-four percent of African-American women have never been married, while 57 percent of white women have been. Only 38 percent of Black children live in two-parent homes. (Essence Magazine, September 2009)** For this reason, the phrase Baby Mama was coined. For some, it's derogatory and for others it's a term of endearment. Our main goal was to get your attention and if you're still reading, we guess it worked.

For some strange reason, people view single mothers as "crazy" baby mamas or typically believe there is baby mama "drama" in our relationships. I can remember several conversations with different men who asked if I was a "crazy" baby mama once they learned I was single with a child. There I was, a college graduate and professional woman being called a Baby Mama. Not too long ago, using the term was an insult (for some it still is). But for the sake of this book, we're speaking to ALL women. Whether you have a child or not, single parents affect us all. Most single women who don't have any children may find themselves dating a man with a child from a previous relationship. Most common are blended families where you will find a couple entering a relationship with children from previous relationships. Various statistics indicate that blended families will be the most common family form in the future. There's no way to avoid it, Baby Mama Drama follows us all.

It's the all-too-familiar-story for everyone: Girl meets Boy. Boy likes Girl.

Girl REALLY likes Boy. Boy and Girl date. Girl and Boy move in together. Girl has baby (or babies) with Boy.

While you're dating, it's usually the most magical period of your relationship. We all want this period to never end because this is where you get to know one another with the expectation of getting into a committed relationship. The wining and dining begins with romantic walks on the beach, candlelight dinners, and constant 'love' text messages. This introduces our "wedding dress" theory. The wedding dress symbolizes our commitment towards our relationships with men and what we expect from them. The key word to be emphasized is *expectations*. It does not mean that you get married, because we all have different expectations. For some the ring and ceremony are important to them but if you've had a child out of wedlock the chances of him asking you to marry him and going through with it is very slim. If you're lucky, you may get an engagement ring but sometimes even that is used as a stall tactic or a F.A.N.M.U (see Chapter Four). You'll hear excuses such as, there isn't enough money to have a wedding or our favorite, "Marriage is just a piece of paper." Most men consider living together and raising a child together a form of marriage but for women, we consider it shacking up. He doesn't understand that you've been planning your entire life ever since you were in kindergarten playing dress up and house. In reality we are playing 'house' as we did as little girls. When we played 'house', there was no wedding but there was a bed and a kitchen. We frantically ran around the kitchen to prepare dinner and the kids for our "husband" because he was on his way home from work at any moment. There was no ring to symbolize the union so why would we expect our children's father to see it any other way.

Once becoming pregnant, our *expectations* (sometimes unrealistic) begin to manifest. We *expect* to have the perfect pregnancy…at least for the first one. We *expect* to deliver naturally without any drugs (that's until the contractions start kicking our butt then it's a different story.) We *expect* for our mate to be at every doctor's appointment for emotional support as both of you watch your child's development. We *expect* that he will be extremely happy with the sex of the child. For instance, if you were expecting a little girl, you pray that he will accept her even if he really wanted a boy. Then, you *expect* to receive lots of gifts from the baby shower, not to worry about money while you're on maternity leave, and have the nursery completed for your baby's first day at home. Finally, it's time for you to go to the hospital and you expect for him to be there the moment you go into labor so that he can drive you and your pre-packed luggage to the hospital.

One way or another, we all *expected* too much from our child's father. For most of us, he probably wasn't in the vicinity of any hospital or the hospital you were admitted in. For Melanie, she almost had to drive herself to the hospital as her son's father was out in the middle of the night clubbing. And my child's father was deciding whether or not he should ask his boss to leave work early because he was put on probation for coming into work late from hanging out late at night with his boys. No matter what your story is, we all *expect* a child to change a man's life. Nevertheless, if your childbirth experience was a positive one, then we applaud you. And if you're still reading this book then most likely you've become a "Crazy" baby mama and you're probably wondering how you became a single mother when everything was going so well.

By the time your child enters the picture, your relationship is either already on the rocks or the series of breaking-up to making-up continues. Aside for Melanie, I can totally relate to the latter because my daughter's father and I broke up so many times during our 10-year relationship that she didn't realize that he was gone for 2 years of her life. It became normal for our daughter to see us get back together.

You *expect* your entire relationship to change once your child arrives. Our expectations of the man who constantly went out with his buddies is suppose to suddenly take his life seriously. Instead, you want him to stay home to help you heal and change diapers in the middle of the night so that you can rest. YEAH, RIGHT! We all wished that happened. Instead, the arguing gets worse, the clubbing becomes more frequent, the finger pointing continues, and the "Crazy" in YOU begins to be exposed either gradually or quickly.

The introduction of the "wedding dress theory" was not to preach to you that you should have been married before having a child because we're sure you got that from someone in your family or one of your friends. To better understand why this theory applies to our lives is for the same reason a woman getting married wants everything to be perfect. Not only does she want it to be a perfect day but she has expectations that it will. She's not concerned that it may rain or she can't afford to buy an expensive dress because this is her day and nothing is going to ruin it. Not all of us wanted marriage with our child's father but we all had *expectations* when it came to the upbringing for our children. We are married to our *expectations* and all the emotions that come with it. It involves our emotional well-being and our *expectations* consume our everyday thoughts whether it is consciously or unconsciously. Just like a wedding ceremony there's the bride and groom, which represents you and your child's father. Your family and friends, who we call the 'wedding party', also volunteers their input and have expectations of their own on your role as a new mother and his role as an expecting father. They are the major players with our theory. How many of us can count the times where our friends or his family members get involved in the arguments that we have with our child's father? Your friends and family *expect* for your child's father to act one way and his family members *expect* for you to behave a certain way especially, as a mother. When this happens we've put on the wedding dress and never take it off until we're ready to let go of a lot of things. Just imagine going through life wearing a wedding dress that symbolizes the emotional baggage single mother's carry and serves as a constant reminder of the struggles, financial hardships, and rejection. You may not realize it but our actions towards our child's father can negatively impact our children if we are not careful with how we handle our emotions. In most cases, we never have the closure to move on. There are far too many of us wearing a wedding dress to work, sleep, while grocery shopping, while we eat, and when going to parent-teacher conferences, not wanting to remove the dress as it will symbolize hurt and pain. By the end of this book we want you to remove your wedding dress so that you can reevaluate your life and revise your list of expectations to be more realistic. In the process you'd be amazed what a difference it will make in your child's life and in YOU!

Chapter 2
Rebuilding Your Relationship With Your Child's Father

At some point in the relationship, we come to realize that the relationship has to end or for some of us, we try to save the relationship for the sake of our child. In *some* cases, saving the relationship works and we stress the word *some*. Not all of us are meant to be with our children's father and that is a reality that's hard to swallow. When you feel defeated in the relationship, your partner picks up on those feelings. If you continue to stay in the relationship feeling that way you must ask yourself, "who are you trying to please?" For most of us, it's fear. Fear of starting all over; Fear of being alone; Fear of proving our family and friends right that you'd end up a baby mama too and Fear of affecting our child's life.

Like us, you may have not planned to have a child with your child's father. In the beginning of the relationship, the men in our lives gave us signs of the type of father he would become. We ignored these signs because we only saw and heard what we wanted to hear and by the time we have children we either continue to ignore the signs or accept him for the man we *want to believe* that he truly is.

I remember asking my daughter's father if he had any kids and he told me flat out "No." Lie #1. Several months later after we began an intimate relationship, he called me to tell me that he was a father. By this time we agreed to start a long distance relationship. He explained that his son's mother cheated on him and he was not sure if the child was his. I was really upset with him for not being upfront with me in the first place. But my lack of experience in a boyfriend-girlfriend relationship and love for him blinded me to the fact

6

he kept this important information from me especially when the topic of children was brought up during one of our many dates. He disrespected me from the beginning and I chose to forgive and forget quickly so that I didn't lose him and try to move on with the relationship. Without saying it, by my actions alone said "I'm going to believe <u>anything</u> and <u>everything</u> you tell me" and lying to me is okay. From that point on, I unknowingly put on my blindfolds and gave my life to the relationship on and off for 10 years.

Almost a year later from the start of our relationship, we decided to move in together. Well, he actually moved in with me. He found a job shortly after that but always expressed that he was not comfortable living with me because it was not truly our own place and we had a roommate. I was in college and my roommate was a male and so there was friction from the start. As in most cases when a man moves into a woman's place, he feels that he does not need to contribute to the household. He figures that everything in your household was fine since you were paying for all the bills on your own prior to him moving in. So why can't those arrangements stay in affect? One mistake I made was moving in a man that never had his own place where he would have learned how to pay his own bills. The lesson that should have been learned is that he showed me from the beginning that he was going to make excuses for everything and anything just so that he can get himself out of taking care of his responsibilities. Just like so many women, I made excuses for his lack of responsibility and stayed in a relationship that was neither productive nor effective for my soul.

Why are we sharing these personal stories with you? It's because we love ourselves so much that we had to give ourselves tough love and we hope you'll do the same for yourself. Even if one of our good friends told us that we were wasting our time with him we would have not listened to them. Like so many single mothers, we go through life making excuses as to why we cannot better our lives. Instead, we continue to make the same mistakes over and over. We don't listen to our hearts and our motherly instincts about the choices we make in our relationships that will ultimately affect our child's upbringing. We may ask for advice about our situation but most of the time we already know the answer. Instead, we hope that our friend or love one that is lending us their ear will tell us what we want to hear. Whatever the case is, sometimes we make decisions based on our emotions and not by what is right or wrong.

At some point in the relationship, you have to consider whether to end the relationship or continue with your child's father. Some experts believe that by the time the child is five years old, both parties determine if they are (if you're lucky) going to stick together or go their separate ways.

When it comes to "sticking together", some of us fall in the category of staying with our child's father for the sake of our child. We want our child to grow up with a father because of the statistics that show children who grow up without a father are likely to become criminals, have psychological issues, or a list of other statistical garbage that is carved into our brains. The most common reason is that we promise ourselves that our child will have a better relationship with their father than we had with our very own. Instead, we remain in the relationship when "things" are not working out. Those "things" could range from the father wanting to continue to live his life as it was prior to having a child and our *expectations* that he must accept his responsibilities based on our perception (sometimes distorted) of how a father should behave. Even though "things" don't get any better, we try to "fix" them so that other people will think that we have our family in order. We "fix" and "fix" and "fix" so that we don't endure embarrassment or ridicule from our family and friends because you don't want to become a statistic by becoming a single mother. We become Super Moms and hide the fact that we're single mothers while in a relationship with the father. We're the ones who will stay home when the child is sick, go to parent-teacher conferences, help with homework, or worse pay all the bills by ourselves. The shame is felt when a family member or friend praises your child's father for accepting responsibility by staying with you and your child and for being a Man. The shame turns into guilt. We begin to feel guilty when we come to the realization that the person we decided to have a child with was not the man we *expected* to have a future with or even worse that he is a S.A.M (See Chapter Four).

You must ask yourself: Is it healthy for you and your child to continue to live in an unhealthy household. Maybe the psychological issues stems from parents living in an unhealthy and unhappy home and those children feed off of the negative energy in their environment. I noticed that once the arguments became worse and I was becoming emotionally stressed, my daughter began to wet the bed again after several months of not wetting the bed. Some people are better off not together than being in a miserable relationship where two people continue to get on each other's nerves.

Staying in an unhealthy relationship can be compared to a bouquet of vibrant colored flowers. Our relationship is the vibrant colored flowers. Now imagine, placing them in a room with no sunlight and no air for three days. It's obvious by the third day the flowers will have become wilted and dead. But with hope, you place those flowers in a beautiful vase with water and an aspirin in front of a window with lots of sunlight. You continue to care for the flowers every other day hoping they will return to the beautiful bouquet of vibrant flowers they once were but they remain dead. Dead like the relationship we're involved in. No air for flowers means no life. Just like

our relationship, we try to bring life back into our bad relationship, but the air has already been sucked from it.

Hopefully rather than stay in a relationship where there is constantly bickering, we figure that it's best to part ways. This is where BOY decides to move back in with his parents or get a place of his own and GIRL becomes a single mother.

Ahhh, the single life: going to clubs, hanging out with friends, and meeting and dating other people. Too bad that's not your new life but it's the new life your child's father has adopted. If we were to participate in any of those extracurricular activities we'd have to find a reliable babysitter at any given notice and monies to pay for their services for each night we go out. Typically, we become full-time mothers with an occasion of taking on fatherly duties like repairing bicycles, playing football with our sons, mowing the lawn, or avoiding any Father & child event. This is where the guilt now becomes anger.

The first year of separation from your child's father is the most challenging. If there is not a set guideline of each parent's responsibility then arguments are expected to increase and the drama and the "Crazy" in YOU begins to unfold. It's extremely difficult when you're living in separate states or don't have family support. Our collection of emotional "*baggage*" accumulates as we feel abandoned by our child's father and we stress ourselves to be the best mom ever. We work every shift available to make extra money so that we can make sure our child never goes without clothes, food, shoes, and school supplies. It becomes natural for us to do this because we are repeating our mother's lives who took on these responsibilities without complaining at all. Most of the time we prefer not to ask our child's father for assistance because we're tired of hearing the word "no" or to prevent an argument or for most of us, we want to show him that we don't <u>need</u> him. Or worse, he calls you and says something stupid like "Why do you always have an attitude with me?" Whatever the reason may be, it can be considered boarder-line selfish on our part. Sometimes we wonder why is it so difficult to develop a healthy and comfortable relationship with someone who has seen our naked bodies? Someone that we loved so much? Someone we considered an important figure in our lives? Someone we shared our most intimate feelings and secrets with? For goodness sakes, someone we had a child with: a little human being who has changed our lives; a miniature replica of ourselves who loves us unconditionally. What if we could go back into time when we were children with hearts full of innocence instead of a heart full of hate so that we can effectively communicate with one another for our child's well being?

Our emotions take the best of us. The longer the relationship was, the harder it is to let go. In most cases, our former partner begins dating other women and expect for us to deal with it respectively. Upon meeting the other women, there is tension. Depending on how good or bad the breakup, there is no telling what he could have told the new woman about you. He could have told her that you have major attitude and when you meet her you prove him right by giving her a dirty look or you don't acknowledge her presence at all. It could be that he called you the day before to tell you that the new woman is a better woman for him than you were. The attitude doesn't stem from her being the new woman it stems from us not being able to let go of our attachment or feelings towards our child's father. No one understands that feeling but a single mother. Outsiders look at us as though we are helpless women who have issues. Instead it's a matter of time we need to deal with our emotions and the steps that we need to prepare ourselves and our children for the new partners that will be introduced to them. Communication is the key factor to let our child's father know how we want to introduce his new partner. It's a difficult step especially when both parents can care less about the other's feelings. We get so caught up with the bickering that we forget that our children can be affected by our actions caused by our reactions. There are outlets that can facilitate the steps to moving on. Whether it's counseling, getting a court approved mediator, or a reliable family member or friend that you both can agree on to eliminate the fighting, you'll definitely make this transition a lot easier.

Chapter 3
The Inner "CRAZY" Baby Mama

Okay, by now you've accepted the fact we all have one or two or three or maybe a lot of "Crazy" moments but let's take a look at some common scenarios we are faced with:

Situation #1: You and your child's father have agreed that he will pay a certain amount of money a week, bi-weekly, or monthly to help you with the costs of your child. Everything seems to be going fine until a month or so passes by and the payments become infrequent and you were counting on the money to help little Johnny get some new sneakers because the one's you bought him less than a month ago that cost $100 (that you didn't have but boys shoes are expensive) somehow don't fit him anymore. You decide to call his father because you feel that you guys were on the right track with communicating with one another and that you can go to him for anything – at least you thought so. He doesn't answer your calls and you leave several messages. He decides to return your call a week later stating that he was busy. Now at this point, your blood starts to boil because you weren't calling to chit chat but for the sake of his child's well being. You begin to tell him the situation with Johnny and he states that he lost his job and can't help you out this month until he gets a job. Then days turn into weeks. Then weeks turns into months. Since all this time has passed, Johnny now needs clothes, a haircut, and a sitter to watch during Spring Break because you have to go to work. You contact his father again and he gets annoyed because you have already told him that he needs shoes months ago and all of a sudden he needs more things. You both get into an argument and he calls you a "greedy bitch" and that's why he's not with your ass anymore.

Resolution: Take in a deep breath and tell him you are going to hang up the phone because one of you has to be an adult in this situation. And since you are already raising one child you don't have time to partake in his childish behavior. I know ladies that may or will be very difficult to say or do but consider all the negative energy in arguing with someone you don't get along with. Go read a book to your child, talk to your child, or do something constructive that can enhance your relationship with him. If you continued arguing with his father on the phone, you are more likely to hold onto that anger and guess who will feel the wrath? You guessed it, your child. It's not Johnny's fault that his feet has jumped two sizes from the previous months. Ask yourself, "does Johnny deserve to be yelled at after moments of a heated argument with his father?" Especially after he hung up on you right before you were going to let him know his mother is really a man. We're sure Johnny will appreciate you for being his provider and will not fully understand why his father can't help you in your time of need. Be thankful for what you have and try not to focus on what you don't have. If your child is healthy, be thankful. If you're healthy, be thankful. If you have a reliable car, be thankful. If you have a roof over your heads, be thankful. The most important person is your child so never lose your focus.

Situation #2: After months of not getting your child's father's cooperation with helping you financially, you decide to go to your local State Attorney's office to file for child support. A year goes by and he is finally served with notice that he must go to court to determine the amount of child support he will be ordered to pay. The first person he calls is, of course, you. When you answer the phone, he doesn't greet you instead he jumps into the topic of the fact you are yet again, a "greedy bitch" who is selfish and doesn't really need assistance but wants extra money to go to the hair salon and get a weekly manicure. This is the same man who during the year the State Attorney was processing your paperwork, did not bother to send you a dime to help Sara get school uniforms for the new school year or school supplies. He rambles on and on about how life is hard for him and he can't seem to pay all his bills.

Resolution: You politely ask him to hold on so that you can check your mailbox. After a few seconds you return to the phone and you let him know that you did not receive his invitation to his pity party and you don't want to be a party crasher so you're going to hang up the phone with him. The best thing to do is to let the courts handle it and if he needs someone to complain to then direct him to his caseworker. If he calls his caseworker, it'll be someone that is getting paid to hear his poor excuses. At that point, you don't have an obligation to him because you wouldn't have taken those measures had he done his part by helping you physically and financially with your child. Everyone has problems and your child is not going to stop growing because there is no money to feed or clothe him. Yet, there are fathers who feel they are the victim. Sarcastically speaking, life is hard for them but not for you. He is experiencing tough times during the recession and acts like you're not in the same recession with him. He can't pay all his bills but you seem to be able to manage with a child. He thinks the system is going to take him for everything he has (which is most likely a video game console and a box of high school memorabilia) because the system was built to work in your favor. It's not worth fighting him when the system is there to help you. It's not for everyone because it does take several months to locate the father even though you provide them his most recent address of residence and sometimes the name and place of where he works. Consider going through the process anyway even if he doesn't provide financial assistance. That way, if at any point in his life he decides to work or win the lottery, you know Uncle Sam has your child in their best interest!

Situation #3: Your child's father starts dating another woman who may or may not have kids of her own. He begins to have your child around this new woman. Every time your child comes home he or she has nothing bad to say about the new girlfriend. But it pains you to see that your child is accepting the new girlfriend or even worse he really likes her (if you have a daughter, she may take longer to warm up to the new woman). Whatever the case may be, you are tempted to enroll your child in every extracurricular activity there is as a way of limiting the time he or she can spend with their father and the new girlfriend.

Resolution: STOP! You have to be a better person and be confident that your child is and will forever be dedicated to you as their mother. No matter how much fun he or she may have with the new girlfriend, remember with the proper guidance (and not manipulation) they will always want to come home to mommy. Instead of contemplating on how you can raise $5000 to send your child to space camp, take the time out for you or hang out with your girlfriends who you have neglected since your child was born. Think of this time away from your child as an advantage and not as a disadvantage. Give the new girlfriend the benefit of the doubt (after you've conducted a criminal background check, interviewed her family, friends, and ex-boyfriends, and checked employment history) and hope for the best that she can possibly make some sort of difference in your child's life. If your child's father has made a commitment to his child by providing child support and spending time with him then there is no need to become vindictive or show your "crazy" side. Remember just be thankful he is doing right unlike some of us who have a S.A.M. in our life.

There may be more examples out there that we may have not mentioned but there are ways to control your inner "crazy". To control the urge of getting yourself into those "crazy" moments it's not going to happen overnight. It takes practice and sometimes sacrifice. Before Max-Laine decided to get into the dating pool, she took three years of alone time to get to know herself again. She lost sight of her dreams and goals because she dedicated her life to her career, child's father, and her child. For a number of years she worked at a dead-end job that wasn't her ideal career choice and you can pretty much predict what happened to her relationship with her daughter's father by reading the title of this book. Other than that, her relationship with her daughter became stronger and she was able to see life from a different perspective. Rather than forgoing those aspirations, she was able to find her passion and pursue her dreams of becoming a writer. She took a negative situation and turned it into a positive one that possibly could help millions of single mothers face their emotions towards their child's father. In later chapters, we will discuss on how you too can make a negative situation into a positive one for you and your child.

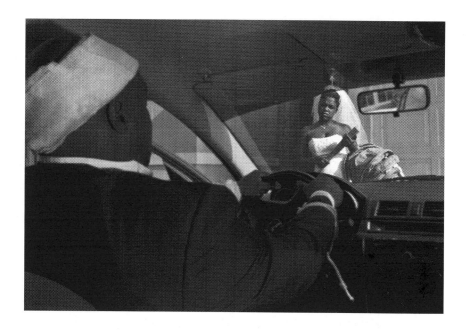

Chapter 4
It Is What It Is

Once we gave birth to our children, we expected their father to change their ways once the nurse puts your child in his arms. We praise the men who step up and should always be encouraged to continue to do so. However, in this chapter we will explore the different kinds of fathers that are out there. Some of us would have not predicted that the outcome of our relationships with our child's father would result in becoming a single mother. Sadly, most of us consider ourselves struggling single mothers but with the right tools we can focus on bettering ourselves to get out of the struggle mode. Below you will find a list that Melanie and I have comprised that will describe the type of men who father our children that are out there. It takes so much more to be a parent to children these days and some men don't get it and very few do. We cannot put blame on a lot of men because they were misguided or didn't have a father figure in their home. So we cannot expect for a misguided man to be the man we need them to be to our children.

F.A.T.H.E.R

This type of man is needed and desired for our children. This is the one who is always there for their child. No matter what, he will provide for his children. He tries his best to have a good relationship with his child's mother. If needed, he will sacrifice working flipping burgers at a fast food restaurant to assure his child has everything he or she needs. This type of individual is worth circling the date for Father's Day on your calendar. He pays child support without a court order. He is there at recitals, award ceremonies, and other special occasions such as birthdays. He will provide for his child without any hesitation or nagging from the mother. Even if there is drama, he will pursue the courts to take action against the mother so that he can continue to be an active parent in their child's life. *Highly desired.*

A.N.D

The term Per Diem is commonly used in the healthcare industry. It relates to when there are not a lot of shifts available and so staff is scheduled on an as needed basis. Some men have adapted this term by telling their child's mother when asked for any type of assistance the catchphrase for him is he can help "when I can." In other words, he's an **As Needed Daddy** so don't hold your breath. Only if he understood that his child is not going to stop growing or eating because he can't provide for them at that moment. Very seldom will he be able to assist you but when he gets some extra money in his pocket and is feeling very generous he'll end up purchasing your child the expensive video game console your child always wanted. The problem is you have a water and power bill that is the same amount of the toy he just purchased. Rather than asking you if you need anything, he purchases this toy because he doesn't have the mental capacity or consideration to ask you what his child needs. If the child is well dressed and fed, the other stuff such as utilities, car note, or rent is not his concern. Although, his child uses those utilities, is transported in your car to and from school, and lives with you 24 hours 7 days a week, his main concern is the child's needs for what he would consider the major necessities such as toys, clothes, & shoes.

S.A.M

As mentioned in a previous chapter, this is when your child's father has proven to be a **Sorry Ass Motherfucker**. This is the lowest level of them all. He has made no attempts to neither help you financially nor spend time with his child. He lives his life as he has no children and when asked for assistance, he provides you with a laundry list of excuses that's if you can reach him. -Opposite of FATHER. -Also known as a Deadbeat Father.

Instant Messenger – LOL!

With the changes of technology and the introduction of various social networking sites and text messages from your cell phone this has given certain fathers another mode of communicating with their children's mom and also with their children. This is the absent father who feels that this is the way that they can communicate and inquire about their child or children. They send messages to "check up" on little Johnny with the mom instead of pushing the "talk" key they click send. Now don't get us wrong some men and women may need to send a message to discuss certain aspects that could be hot topics and turn into an argument but they should never send text messages or messages via other social networking outlets to find out how their children are doing – especially when they do not communicate or even attempt to see their children.

F.A.N.M.U

Fiancée is a common term that is used immediately after a child is born out of wedlock. Most woman use this term too loosely because they are ashamed to be considered as a single mother and suddenly becomes 'wifey'. At this point, the child's father is *expected* to propose or someday make the commitment to his newly made family. Most of the time there is no engagement ring to symbolize the anticipated union just conversations initiated by the child's mother who out of embarrassment want to marry her child's father. Our focus is not to single mothers who eventually married their child's father but to those who *expect* a marriage to occur. If years have passed where there is no marriage and more children are born, this term should not be used because ***Fiancée Ain't Never Marrying U***. This not only confuses your child but is a huge disappointment to us when our *expectations* are not met. Hint: If your child's father has promised marriage and does not make efforts to marry you and continue having children then at some point please re-evaluate your relationship. The most common excuse used by the couple is that they are waiting to save their money so that they can have a nice wedding ceremony. If that is the case, going to the justice of the peace is a better option while saving for it. Also see The Manipulator.

M.A.T.T

Manipulators Always Talk Trash is a man who has two or more children with two or more women. If this man isn't with his first child's mother, we can easily provide the excuse that "things" just didn't work out. The first relationship is where there are mistakes made and we can all agree that the child is not the mistake. As he moves to the next relationship, this is the one that matters and determines what type of man he really *is*. This is his chance to be in a nurturing relationship where he can grow and learn from his past mistakes from his previous relationship. To make matters more difficult he has to sustain a relationship with his child from the previous relationship and maintain the peace with their mother. With the new mate, she has to be understanding and patient. Things get stickier once the new mate gets pregnant. Depending on the relationship he has with the first child's mother will determine how the news of him having another child with someone else will be received. In this case, the Manipulator doesn't really have a good relationship with the previous mother so expectantly she will not accept this news with an open heart. Once the second relationship with The Manipulator's child's mother is over, he then has to juggle between the mothers and children. The younger the children are the more he has to handle where he evolves as a Manipulator. Have you ever wondered why the children's mothers end up arguing or have an altercation? Yep, you guessed it's because the Manipulator facilitated the tension between them so that he can redirect any attention towards him to the drama that has unfolded. The more mothers and children there are the more complicated his situation gets and there is no perfect situation. Somewhere there is drama whether big or small, it never goes away. As The Manipulator continues to date more women, he has to present himself as Prince Charming because more women will be turned off by his 'situation' once it's revealed (if he even discloses that information) that he has children. He will woo the heck out of a woman so that she can feel "lucky" to be with him and that the other women were fools for letting him go. He has succeeded once the woman has accepted him and his 'situation'. If there is any tension or anger towards the new woman, an evaluation is in order. It can be that The Manipulator has told one mother one thing and the other something totally different. Most likely he will tell the new woman that the others are jealous of her and they regret that "things" didn't work out for the better with him. Leaving the woman to believe that she has someone that everybody wants and continues to build further a relationship with him. As the single mother in this situation, there are sides to her story as well. In some cases, The Manipulator hasn't ended one relationship only leaving the mother to believe that they will get back together. To keep the peace, he will string her along probably telling her that the new woman means nothing to him. There is no way of determining what is being said and how The Manipulator actions affect the mother's involved. He is also considered a Magician because he will make you see things that are not there and that his faults are not his fault. If you are making excuses for him then he is winning you over. For example, if he doesn't have a job then he will make it seem that he is trying his best to get out of the situation and you will end up feeling sorry for him. If he doesn't have a job, he just doesn't have a job. What you are saying to him is that you justify his situation. Also, he is very fearful of people who have common sense, especially if they are your friends or loved ones. He is fearful that they will see him for who he truly is and that they will make you realize this revelation. The Manipulator is a master at his craft that he will cause any distraction so that you will not interact with this person. If he is aware of any friends or family members that do not like him then you will probably not interact with them because he will make you believe that that person has a problem with themselves rather than with him.

Before you go to the mountaintop screaming what you consider your child's father to be, realize you can't determine the type of father he is if he doesn't do things the way you want him to. Too many women abuse their authority and try to make their child's father suffer. When we're no longer with them we *expect* them to play by our rules and be there whenever we need them. The most annoying type of single mother is the one that will not allow her child to see their father especially when he gets the court involve. We need more men to accept their responsibilities and the ones that are responsible are rare to find. It is not the time to act a fool and keep your child away from their father unless yours or their life is in danger and don't use that as an excuse if it's not true. We all want to consider our child's father as a deadbeat and call him S.A.M. every time we see him but give him an opportunity to be the father he thinks he should be. Now is not the time to try to change him since he didn't change when you were with him. It's not about you or him; it's about your child. We can't assume that our children don't understand and we can't protect them from everything. You'd be amazed how children pick up on your actions as well as their father and interpret it in their own childlike reasoning without any explanations. If they have an absent father, they may shut down where they will no longer ask for their whereabouts after not hearing from them for a long period of time. No amount of explanations can make them understand adult behavior. We are not therapists but we are nurturers and must do what comes natural for our children by providing them love. Single mothers should try to make reasonable efforts to encourage (not discourage) their children's father to be in their lives. The fact that there are women who are abusing the child support system doesn't help. There are child support cases where the father is ordered to pay an exuberant amount of money monthly and this will deter men from accepting their responsibilities to their child. It hasn't been until recently that men are fighting for their rights and they should have an opportunity to do so especially if the mother isn't doing a good job of raising their child. Put yourself in their shoes. Most of these deadbeat fathers were not raised by their fathers and were not taught to be responsible. In retrospect, our mothers taught us to be strong women so that we would not depend on a man for anything. This prepared many of us to self-sabotage our own relationships with men because we imitate our mother's attitude and behavior.

Chapter 5
More Crazy Baby Mama's....

Although we've redefined what a "Crazy" Baby Mama is the following people in this news article in our opinion go far and beyond what we are talking about......and yes it really happened. (Please note that we have removed the names of all parties named in this article)

Women's clash led to 6 carloads of people at brawl
Kids present as two people shot, 11 arrested
Hollis, J, Morris, M, The Atlanta Journal-Constitution, *March 2009*

Fulton County police said a melee that erupted outside a south Fulton residence early Tuesday morning was part of an ongoing conflict between two women who have children by the same man.

Two men were wounded and 11 people were arrested, said Fulton County police spokeswoman FEMALE OFFICER.

FEMALE OFFICER said the fracas started about 12:45 a.m. Tuesday on Westford Circle off Old National Highway at the residence of FEMALE #1, (age) 28. FEMALE #1 and FEMALE #2, (age) 20, both have children by a man police identified as BABY DADDY. FEMALE #1 said he'd just left her house when the conflict occurred. FEMALE #2 could not be reached for comment Tuesday night.

According to FEMALE #1, FEMALE #2 showed up at her house and the two women fought. FEMALE #2 returned a short time later, saying she had lost her cellphone, FEMALE #1 said.

Later, FEMALE OFFICER said, "Ms. FEMALE #2 drove to Ms. FEMALE #1 residence with approximately six carloads of people wanting to fight."

Shortly after that battle began, the two groups exchanged gunfire.

SUSPECT #1, (age) 22, and SUSPECT #2, (age) 30, were wounded by gunfire, FEMALE OFFICER said. Both men were in stable condition at Grady Memorial Hospital.

"There were many juveniles on the scene at the time the gunfire was exchanged," FEMALE OFFICER said, adding that one of the vehicles that drove to the scene had about eight children inside, ranging in age from one to nine.

Charges against the 11 included aggravated assault, battery, disorderly conduct and cruelty to children. FEMALE #2 was among the people charged.

Chapter 6
Baby Mama vs. Child's Mother

Let's face it, in the beginning the phrase baby mama was a derogatory term and now society has embraced it. It has crossed over and national journalists and bloggers alike have taken this phrase to describe a presidential candidate's wife as his baby mama and Hollywood made millions off the same title by turning it into a movie. No matter how you look at it being a baby mama is a state of mind and just because we have had a child (or a few) out of wedlock does not mean we must carry ourselves as such. There are so many names that people have used that will provoke them to become upset. But as a Nigerian professor taught me, he said that hurtful words that are directed to you are only effective if the target feels that those words are true. For instance, if someone were to call me a Black Bitch, I would be more insulted about the black part than the bitch word because I don't consider myself as a bitch. That lesson taught me that hurtful words will always be used and never goes away so why let them affect me. Yes, it's difficult to ignore someone being disrespectful but what do you accomplish when you curse, spit, or tear off a wig....NOTHING! The amount of negative energy used on someone that is probably not worth being upset for could be used for something positive. You're giving that person control over your emotions and our point is to make you realize that when you're having an argument with your child's father it affects you more than him. Men don't react the same way we do so after a heated argument he probably leaves and cools down after a couple of hours. What we do as women and single mothers is that we internalize those feelings of anger and never forgive or forget that incident. He goes to bed that night only to wake up with little memory of what occurred the night before and you've been up tossing and turning replaying the words yelled at one another. We want him to walk around being hurt as we are, he probably is but his actions are not going to be what we *expect* them to be. Being upset with bags under your eyes indicating another sleepless night only affects how you're going to make it through your day. Imagine how that will affect not only your mind but your body because now you're going to still be mommy, co-worker, friend, sister, customer and the million roles we play on a daily bases. So embrace being a great mother regardless if people call you a baby mama, just politely say no, I'm his child's mother.

Chapter 7
Get Uncomfortable

One day as my hair stylist, Darryl, prepared to curl my hair he suddenly turned the chair around and looked straight into my eyes and asked me if I was okay. It was a cold and gloomy day and the sky was so dark that not a hint of sunshine appeared through the gray clouds. I was dressed in an old sweater and baggy jeans covering a pair of ripped up knee-highs (shh don't tell anyone) with an old pair of mules. I found it odd for him to ask this question especially after turning the chair to speak directly to me. I hesitated, thinking that it was a trick question. Slowly the words left my mouth, "Yeah." He then asked with a puzzled look, "Are YOU sure?" Now he was really making me question myself. Things were going great…at least I thought. I had a decent job, my daughter thankfully was healthy, and I had recently moved in with my mother so that I could get back on my feet. It wasn't my ideal situation but I felt any day not being in a dead end relationship was doing GREAT in my book. Darryl had good intentions when he asked me that question THAT day. By then, I had known him for a couple years and well your hair stylist is sometimes your therapist too. He felt the need to tell me that I needed to take a look at myself. That was easy there was a full-length-mirror in front of us. If you're like me, I hate rainy days and if it could be a law placed for the city to shut down on those days I'd be the first person in line to vote for it. So this day even though I was getting primped and pampered I still chose this old black faded sweater and blue jeans that were as baggy as Darryl's jeans (which he pointed out that a woman's jeans should NOT be baggy instead it should flatter your figure not hide it). But of course I didn't see anything wrong with this because I figured once my hair was styled that I should be ok and trying to be cute walking in high heels in the rain is not my thing. Then he began picking my outfit apart and lectured me on how I needed to take better care of myself. What? Are you kidding me? There I was sitting in front of him a refreshed woman on her way to fulfilling dreams that were deferred…so I thought. Without missing a beat I said, "I'm comfortable." Darryl's eyes grew larger and began shaking his head. The words that came out of his mouth next have been embedded in my mind ever since that day. He said with care, "Max-Laine, get Uncomfortable!"

After getting out of a relationship, we all fall or stay in our comfort zone. At that time I was a prime example of that. I could have easily picked out a better outfit that day because I had just purchased a couple of new outfits that I was saving for the next time I was going "out" or for a special occasion. Just had Darryl explained it to me, I was "out" getting my hair done and that was an opportunity for me to dress up. When I do dress up, I feel like a new person with so much confidence. An old saying says, "You look good, You feel good, You feel good, You do good." I was so wrapped up in getting my life together that I neglected the most important person and that was Me.

It's hard raising a child on your own and dealing with all the struggles of doing that and when you mix in personal and financial issues it's easy to forget about ourselves. We get consumed in making a better life for our children and the sad part is that our physical health and emotional well-being suffers as well. The inner circle which consists of our family members, co-workers and friends will never see this because we present ourselves as strong woman who have everything under control. The reality is that we're broken women trying to survive every day. Our hearts have been broken; our mindset has been reprogrammed; our lives have shifted.

Once our child is born, our lives shift into overdrive. No longer can we be the selfish individuals that could pick up and go out in the middle of the night to get something to eat. The days of hanging out with friends in the middle of the week to grab a drink which turns into a night on the town and getting home moments before your alarm clock wakes you up for work are just fade to black memories.

Our motherly instincts quickly set in and our focus is on the screaming newborn baby crying two in the morning to be fed as you try your best to get out of the bed fast enough even though the stitches from the caesarian delivery hasn't healed.

Most of our thoughts and habits are learned from our parents. Especially, if we were raised in a single parent household. Meaning, we were raised to be single-minded adults. If we don't take the initiative to get uncomfortable, we will become bitter old women living in a house by ourselves angry at the world blaming it for our failures...like our mothers did.

Chapter 8
Code of Ethics for Single Mothers (MOM-mandments)

Don't let a man move in with you. <u>Reason</u>: If you allow a man to move in with you that has never had a place of his own then you're more likely to obtain more responsibilities than before. If he has never had his own place prior to moving in with you it shows his lack of responsibility and immaturity because he may not understand your duties of being a single mother and that in turn will affect your relationship. It's almost like adopting another child because now you have another mouth to feed, your utility bills will go up, you'll spend more in gas, and you'll endure more stress. If he is immature or inexperienced, his mentality will be "hey you were paying bills on your own before I moved in, why can't you continue to do so while I'm here." It's better if you have separate homes or (only if necessary) you move in with your mate. You know your limitations and pretty much know how to run a household and if anything goes wrong in your relationship then you'll be able to start over on your own without any hesitation.

Don't allow his dreams become your dreams. <u>Reason:</u> As single mother's we sacrifice our dreams so that we can provide for our children. We put off going back to school to obtain our degrees when we're only a few credits away from graduation or starting our own business because we're afraid to fail. We can easily jump on board of our mates' dreams because we strive to build a partnership with them. When this happens we can become vulnerable to their needs to make their dreams a reality, in which can lead to stress in the relationship if it doesn't happen. Be cautious of going through life unable to fulfill your wants and desires for someone else's dreams. Remember, you must have your own life when you're in a relationship because you or your mate shouldn't feel claustrophobic within your relationship.

Don't change for him. Reason: Be You! At some point of our lives we have to accept who we are. We all can change a few things we don't like about ourselves but it should not be for our significant other. Once we try to change for someone else you are giving them power over you. It's almost like they're your puppet master. You may be thinking, who would change for a man but trust us there are women out there that will or sadly have changed for their man.

Don't start dating immediately after a breakup. Reason: Speaking from experience, we highly recommend to wait at least six months to a year after a break-up. Depending on the length of the relationship, it may take up to a year to get yourself together. This will allow you to reevaluate all of your past relationships and allow your heart and mind to heal. You don't want to rush into another relationship to make the same mistakes from previous relationships. Although, we want to consider ourselves as the perfect mate let's face it nobody is perfect so don't play yourself. Otherwise, your home will be a revolving door of men coming in and out of your children's lives. Too many children have Uncle-Daddies that were exes of single mother's and this confuses children. They'll be exposed to relationships that lack commitment and responsibility. Allow your child to see you as a different person from your previous relationship. Your child will notice how happier or unhappy you are in the new relationship because they'll have another relationship to compare it to.

Don't be afraid of child support. Reason: So many women refuse to put their child's father on child support for reasons that can be considered as lame excuses. The child support system was placed to make absent parents accountable for their child's well-being. We don't condone woman who abuse the system to milk their child's father for every penny they have. We're merely saying that child support is to help you with the daily needs such as clothing, food, and school supplies. Even if you know he will not pay, put it in place so that in the event he comes into a large sum of money you know your child will be provided after Uncle Sam takes his cut. Be aware of your child father talking you into dropping the case. If he never discussed giving you support until he was served with the papers then what makes you think that he is willing to do so now. Keep in mind, the child support process can be very lengthy in some states and if you drop the case only to have to reapply makes it more difficult on you and more time for him to run from the system.

Don't allow your child's father to get you upset. Reason: For your child's sake, you should not allow them to see you get upset when speaking to their father. There are other ways to communicate so that this will not happen. Technology has allowed us to eliminate face-to-face or verbal contact with one another. If you see that you're getting angry, hang up the phone and send a kind text message stating that you will call him back so that both of you can cool down. For others, the moment we have to communicate to our child's father our blood pressure rises, breathing becomes faster, and our fists may clinch. This is the best time to have a mediator who will not take sides and is only there to communicate through. That person should be able to effectively relay messages that will not cause the other person to get angry.

Don't always listen to your single-mother friends or single girlfriends. Reason: Listening to other single mother's issues with their children's father only makes your situation worse. If you insist on listening to another single mother's struggle, it's best to have a woman who is more than 10 years older than you who will save you 10 years of mistakes. We found that speaking to women who are older or wiser than you can shed some light on the experiences you have dating and your relationship with your child's father. We may have lived in a different time than woman who are older than us but you will find that they are wiser and have better insight on the life we're living now. We don't suggest this friend be your mother (unless you have that kind of honest relationship with her) but someone who you will not consider her motherly advice to be over bearing as it would if it came from your own mother. After the age of 50, women are most likely settled in their life where their own children are living their own lives and they have no shame to share their past experiences with men, money, and sex. It is what it was and they are past the stage of making excuses for their actions. Most likely, these women have experienced what you are going through even if it was a different era. We've found that this type of relationship is rewarding because you not only have someone that is going to be truly honest with you but someone you can learn from that will help you in becoming a better YOU.

Don't neglect your parental responsibilities while dating. <u>Reason:</u> Many of us get excited when we're dating someone new. It's like we're fifteen all over again. We want our new beau to perceive us as a strong single woman first and not as a struggling to pay the bills kind of mother. We'll easily try to present ourselves in the best light possible so that our beau won't run off to find someone else. If he is going to accept you for who you are then he is going to have to accept your child as well and the duties that come along with it. There is no reason why we have to present ourselves as though we don't have any issues and that our world is perfect. Whether he has a child or not, you have the responsibility to your child first and no relationship should come between that or your child will eventually blame you for neglecting them. The best way to see if he can handle your situation is to see how he reacts to you spending time with your child rather than spending time with him. If he acts annoyed, then you need to serve him his walking papers.

Don't be bitter, be better. <u>Reason:</u> Being angry at your child's father is not healthy for your child. Many times we hold on to the anger and act out our emotions where it causes an argument and stirs up more drama. When you're around him and you're mad, it only gives him power. You're proving him right when he calls you out by calling you "crazy." It's easy to say 'he provokes me' but you're a grown ass woman who should know better. For instance, when he picks up your child, keep the conversation at a minimum. Say hello, pass him your child's things that he/she will need while there with him, and keep it moving. He won't know what to think. He'd be amazed that there wasn't any drama and will follow your lead. It boils down to control, you want things to go your way and he wants things to go his way. If you allow yourself to be bitter, you're focusing to much attention on the negative. It prevents you from meeting the right person because you'll assume that all men are the same way. Your relationship with your ex will let your next mate know how you are in relationships. If there is so much drama in your past relationship, then it's safe to assume you'll bring that drama and cause new drama with him too. For goodness sake, let it go and get yourself ready for the next relationship.

Don't tell them, teach them: The best thing you can do when you want someone to do what you want them to do is to teach them. For instance, if someone is all up in your business and you tell them to stay out of your business that'll make them want to know more of your business. Instead, when that someone tries to get information from you just ignore them and change the subject about them, say okay, anything but a reaction to it. That's what they want to see is a reaction. Any type of reaction will do because that'll give them fuel to keep their nose in your business. At some point they will see that they can't get any more information from you and they'll eventually leave you alone.

BONUS:

Don't hear him but listen to him: Often times, we hear what people say. When you hear someone, you're likely to hear what you want to hear. But when you listen, you will listen to every word. For instance, one date said to me, 'I want to date and have fun before I get married.' The old me would have heard him say, 'I want to date YOU until WE get married.' About a month later, I found out that I was the "fun" he was referring to because he told me nonchalantly that he got engaged soon after our date. Far too many times, we misconstrue what men say to us because our mindset is misconstrued. If you put too much emphasis on looking for the man of your dreams instead of taking the time to let things happen naturally, you're setting up yourself to feel rejected. And remember when you're speaking, someone may be *listening* to you too.

These are just a few suggestions you should consider when preparing yourself for your next relationship. Maybe we should choose our men like we do our careers. When you're looking for a job, depending on your experience, you may be very picky in choosing the right job for you. You'll research the company, ask lots of questions during the interview, and still apply with other companies before you make your final decision. Write a list of the 'realistic' qualities you want in a mate so you'll have a better strategy in making the right decisions in all aspects of your life.

Chapter 9
Hustle Mentality

As a single mom your motivation changes, your attitude changes, and overall life changes. I knew that I had to make things happen and make them happen quickly. I had to figure out how I was going to raise my son and how to balance my career. I had to keep the career moving in a positive way and not let the ball drop especially since I receive no assistance from my son's father. Even though my son's father stated that he would help me financially that eventually faded away like the relationship we once had. The only reason why he started to assist was when I filed the child support paper work. Once I decided to drop the filing he stated that he would continue to assist "as much as possible" well that promise was of course broken so now I'm facing the court with my papers again to move forward to have them force him to take care of his son.

The question I ask myself everyday is how did I end up being a one parent situation? How did I end up, now 6 years later, raising my son by myself? Why is it that his father calls once every blue moon to even ask about how his son is doing? How is that he can continue to have more children and he doesn't even take care of his son? I know some of you may be asking the same questions about your situations but just know that you are not alone. There are many of you that are walking in the same shoes as Max-Laine and I are now walking. I come from a single parent household in which my mother was my caretaker and provider so it seems that I have ended up in the same cycle. The only difference is that my mother actually walked down the aisle with her wedding dress and became a wife but we both ended up in the same role – single mom – sole provider.

Once my relationship ended I was left with a ton of responsibilities that I really was not ready for but I faced them and basically got into hustle mode. I had to make sure that the bills were paid and that I could provide for my son and that meant taking on additional jobs and that also meant to start working on a bigger plan so that doors could be opened in the future. I started working on my Master's degree. At first it sounded great – but what was even better was that I could get an additional check to supplement my income from student loans. Now getting loans wasn't the best plan (since I was racking up bills for the future) but it was an easy plan and at the same time I was improving my future. I took classes online and also travelled to the campus when required. I made it work for me and I knew that I could make my future brighter. Now not every single mom may take this route – I know some single mom's that have worked at clubs for adult entertainment and some that work two and three jobs to make ends meet. At the end of the day – they all had a hustle mentality and just knew that they had to sacrifice for their children.

Stripping never came to my mind but ladies I understand why that's an option. I actually use to sell designer bags in the strip club to dancers to make quick side money. You may ask why the strip club – well strippers get paid cash so there was no excuse such as "Do you take debit cards or checks?" I would bring them what they wanted in the latest bags and they would have the cash. Hustler mommies understand that they have to think outside of the box and provide for their families immediately especially if you're the only one providing. See what many baby daddies don't understand is - mothers will go through hell and high water to make sure that their children are fed, sheltered, and educated.

Chapter 10
RETHINK...REDO...REVITALIZE

Once the relationship ended and the dust settled the reality of life sank in. I was now on my own raising my son and trying to understand how I got to this point in my life. I still had my wedding dress on and wore it everywhere I went – to the grocery store, to the mall, to my friend's houses, to work, and I even wore it to the strip clubs while I was selling bags. I still carried the emotional baggage and still held on to my past life hoping that the hands of time would rewind and things would go back to how it used to be. I didn't want to consider myself a "baby mama" because that was a statistic and "I'm not a statistic." Yeah, right – I'm number 152,002 of that statistic! Then add the term "crazy" in front of the word "baby mama" then you have a common term that is thrown around within the black community to label that usually describes a woman that acts out towards her child's father in a negative way. Acting out in such ways as: attempting to stab or shoot your child's father, slashing car's tires, keying cars, smashing windshields and windows with a brick, stalking your child's father at the club or at their new girlfriend's house. That's just crazy – you have so much more to focus on – first priority is to focus on yourself and the second priority is your children.

RETHINK

If you are wearing your symbolic wedding dress, it is now time to RETHINK why you are still wearing that dress. It is time to reset expectations for your life and for your child or children. Start to RETHINK how you are going to interact with your child's father in which the relationship does not have a negative impact on your child or yourself. Children react either negatively or positively based on the relationship mom and dad has with each other and with them. If you are in a negative relationship with your child's father is it because you have expectations of still being in a toxic relationship, is it because he is not fulfilling his part in being a father to your child? Whatever the answer maybe, you are the one that has to take a stand. You have to make the decision to back away from the toxic relationship no matter how hard that may be – you have to RETHINK the type of relationship you want your child to be exposed to and you have to RETHINK the type of relationship you want for yourself. You are not the only one that has come to this crossroad in life, many of us can relate. As I always say to Max-Laine – I have heard the same story told by so many different women but yet the story is always the same. RETHINK the life you want for yourself and your children – start now!

REDO

I would always joke with my friends and family and say that I want a REDO in life. They would always ask me what would I REDO? My answer would be to follow the "red flags" that were waving in my face during the relationship I had with my son's father. Shoulda, coulda, woulda are the famous words that I use to say in my times of being angry and frustrated. The REDO that Max-Laine and I focus on now is making different choices to have different outcomes. Right now I'm in the spiritual and physical REDO of my life. Spiritually I knew that I was lacking and I knew that if I had focused more on my connection to God then I would have made better choices in my life – but that's where the shoulda, coulda, woulda words come into play. Every day is an opportunity to learn and grow spiritually. Every day is a battle – to make the right choices and to keep myself grounded because the urge to turn on the "crazy" baby mama switch occurs more often than I would like – not because I am not done with that relationship – it's because I feel that I am the one left with such a huge responsibility of raising a human being on my own without even the concern from his father. Why is that men (and in some instances women) just leave their children without even turning back to wonder how they are doing?

Physically I felt like I let myself go and used the excuse of I didn't have time but really I just wasn't motivated.

REVITALIZE

By the time this book is published, our homes would have foreclosed, Max-Laine lost her job and car was repossessed, we would have filed for bankruptcy, both our children's fathers continued to default on their responsibilities to them, and we incurred more student loan debt.

As single moms, we have to endure so much that we don't have time to breakdown to cry. Instead, we have to *keep it moving* and don't think about how it is affecting us emotionally because we have to find quick resolutions to problems that haven't occurred yet. We're always *expecting* the worst and if things turn out good then we're not confident that it'll last long. We are so use to disappointments that we do not have any confidence when it comes to men keeping their word, whether they are just dating you or if they're your child's father. Sometimes we wonder why things can't be easy. If our children's father would just understand that the smallest gesture makes the world of a difference. A simple phone call often to tell their child they love them would mean a lot not only to us but to their child. When they promise us or kids something and they don't follow through it makes us angry rightfully so. It makes matter worst when they don't understand why we're mad at them. When this occurs so often, we become numb. That's where we were by the time we started writing this book. (For those of you who have children under five years old, you probably will not understand that statement. It's because your child is so young and the wounds are fresh.) By the time our children turned five years old, we were ready to move on to something and someone else because we finally were able to let go of the relationships with their fathers and all of the drama that came with it.

Get uncomfortable single moms! It's time to REVITALIZE your spirit, dreams, and old and new relationships. Look up at the sky and not down at your feet when you're walking down the street. Hold your head up high. Do you know who you are or could be? Release those old thoughts that prevent you from moving forward to become a healthier and happier you. Prove to yourself that there lives inside of you someone who deserves respect, love, and the right to live the life you want for yourself and your child. Don't doubt yourself; Don't limit yourself; and Don't make any more excuses. The time is now!

There is no right way to end this book because we're not the first or the last ones to become a single mother. Our goal is to start discussions and spark debates so that we can find the best way to resolve this epidemic of the abandonment of children by their fathers. Not all mothers are the same and we understand that. We know what worked best for us may not work for you. Finding a way to take off the wedding dress will not only begin your life in a new direction but your child will benefit too. We've learned to laugh at the "crazy" baby mama comments because it is a state of mind. We are no longer allowing those words to define who we are. We've branded ourselves and named our company "Crazy" Baby Mamas because we've learned to embrace and love the "crazy" baby mama in us and we hope you will too. So the next time someone asks, "Are you a "crazy" baby mama?", tell them 'YES' because you're "crazy" about yourself and your child(ren).

Remember to RETHINK, REDO, & REVITALIZE. Once you do, everything else will fall into place.

To:
Newton S., Xuchilt, Tanisha C., Joanna W.G., Vera M., Hamlet Junior, Ghislaine A., John C., D.S.T., & Family and Friends.

we say THANK YOU!!

Book Club Questions:

1. What is your definition of a "Crazy" Baby Mama?

2. Now that you have read this book, do you think you need to make changes in your life so that you can have a better relationship with your child's father? Why or why not?

3. Why do you think men who are considered "deadbeat" dads abandon their responsibilities for their children?

4. What are some challenges single mothers face when dating?

5. What are some advantages and disadvantages in dating a single mom?

The 30 Day "Crazy" Baby Mama Challenge

The 30-Day "Crazy" Baby Mama Challenge Workbook

It's time to Let It Go! For the next 30 days, challenge yourself to become a BETTER YOU! Don't start tomorrow, start now! YOU deserve to live your life emotionally free from the hurt and pain you have encountered throughout the years. Sometimes, the pain you hold onto is the very thing that will hold you back from experiencing the life you have always dreamed of. Writing can be a very healthy way to heal and it will allow you to document your growth physically, mentally, emotionally, and spiritually.

Be Honest! No one can do it for you but YOU. By the end of the *30-Day "Crazy" Baby Mama Challenge*, we encourage you to stay focused on your goals and stay true to yourself. Good Luck!

Direction: The following pages will guide you to become a better YOU. Each page will include a special thought or reminder followed by questions to help you start writing. Don't limit yourself by trying to answer the questions, instead use it as YOUR guide. Go at your own pace but be consistent and make every effort to complete the workbook so that you will be able to implement what you've learned into your life.

Let's Begin!

Day One

Spending time with your child is very important. This may not be so much of a challenge because we are always *with* our children. Being with your child is not the same as *spending time* with them. Take a moment to let your child know that they are important. Before you begin this journey, realize WHO is important to you. Our children sometimes get mixed in the shuffle while we try to balance our careers and our duties as a mom. Allow this moment to put things into perspective so that you can open your heart and mind to a *new* way of living your life.

How often do you say, "I Love You?" How affectionate are you towards your child? Has your child ever seen you argue with their father? Have you ever had a discussion with your child about their father? Was it a positive or negative discussion? How does your child feel about your relationship with their father?

_____
_____
_____
_____
_____
_____
_____
_____
_____
_____
_____
_____
_____
_____
_____
_____
_____
_____
_____
_____

DAY Two

BREAK A BAD HABIT

Don't think about your typical 'bad habit' like biting your nails. Go deeper. For instance, revaluate your relationship with your child's father. What were some of YOUR past or current bad habits that you would like to change? Think of the ones that you DON'T want to repeat in your next relationship?

What is your bad habit? Why do you think it's important to break your bad habit? How does it make you feel?

_____
_____
_____
_____
_____
_____
_____
_____
_____
_____
_____
_____
_____
_____
_____
_____
_____
_____
_____
_____
_____
_____
_____
_____
_____

DAY Three

Need a Financial Breakthrough? Every day is a struggle to make sure our finances are in order so that our children have the things that they need. Determine how you can be better when it comes to your finances. Learn new ways to get out of the habit of living pay check to pay check or control your spending. Plan to get out of debt by making a list of realistic goals.

How would you feel if you lost your job, home, and career today? Why? What are the THINGS you can live without? How do you feel when you do not have any money? What are you teaching your child about money? What are you going to do differently to make your finances better?

_____
_____
_____
_____
_____
_____
_____
_____
_____
_____
_____
_____
_____
_____
_____
_____
_____
_____
_____
_____
_____
_____
_____

DAY Four

Have you ever thought of trying something new but always talked yourself out of doing it? Maybe you thought 'it's too late or I'm too old.' Have you ever heard of the phrase, *It's Never Too Late?* Live outside yourself for just one day. Be the person YOU envisioned yourself becoming. Don't limit yourself by putting pressure to succeed. The BEST part of trying something new is *TRYING*.

What is the ONE thing you would like to try? Why has is taken you so long to do this? What are your fears? How do you plan to overcome those fears? When are you going to TRY something new?

_____
_____
_____
_____
_____
_____
_____
_____
_____
_____
_____
_____
_____
_____
_____
_____
_____
_____
_____
_____
_____
_____

DAY Five

The most rewarding way you can feel appreciated is through donating your time to an organization that you are passionate about. No matter what you are going through someone in the world is going through harder times than you are. It can be very difficult at times to think that no one can understand what you are going through. You may feel like you are the only one and you would be very surprised to find out that you're NOT.

What organization or cause are you passionate about? Can you donate something that's special to you? Has someone ever done anything nice for you? What was it? How did it make you feel? How are you going to donate your time? When are you going to complete this challenge? How do you feel when you GIVE something to someone?

_____

_____

_____

_____

_____

_____

_____

_____

_____

_____

_____

_____

_____

_____

_____

_____

_____

_____

_____

_____

_____

DAY Six

Have a "ME" Day. Often time's single moms never take a moment to be by themselves. We are always with other people. Step away from your duties by doing something you enjoy. There are always moments for "ME" time. Don't feel guilty for wanting some time for yourself. It's an opportunity to RE-juvenate your mind and spirit. Most importantly, it allows you to RElease some stress.

How often do you have "ME" days? What type of activities do you enjoy doing? When is the best time to schedule a "ME" Day? Have you ever enjoyed an activity by yourself? How will it make you feel spending time by yourself?

DAY Seven

Dream Big! Everyone has dreams but to pursue those dreams as a single mom can be unattainable only if YOU allow this statement to be true. Many of us put off our dreams because we focus more on raising our children. Don't wait until your child is grown to pursue your dreams. Start now! Be cautious and don't share your dreams with everyone. Sadly, there are people that may discourage you from moving forward with pursuing your dream. They may mean well but all they are doing is feeding you more fear. You can buy that home you've been dreaming about or go back to school to get your degree. Whatever your dreams are YOU can accomplish them just as long as you create the right *Plan of Action for YOU*!

> *What are your dreams? Which dream is more realistic to pursue? How long will it take you to accomplish your goal of fulfilling this dream? How will it make you feel once you fulfill your dream?*

_____
_____
_____
_____
_____
_____
_____
_____
_____
_____
_____
_____
_____
_____
_____
_____
_____
_____
_____
_____
_____
_____

DAY Eight

Keep up your appearance by pampering yourself. When you look good, you'll feel good. So many single moms let themselves go and allow their self-esteem to suffer as well. It doesn't cost a lot to look good. You can do so much for so little. There are ways to exercise on your own without paying gym fees and most department stores cater to our small budgets when it comes to fashion. It's about being creative with what you *do* have instead of what you *don't* have. GO FOR IT by sprucing up an old pair of your favorite shoes with a HOT affordable purse.

How do you feel about your appearance? Do you like exercising?
What are some ways you can stay fit?

_____
_____
_____
_____
_____
_____
_____
_____
_____
_____
_____
_____
_____
_____
_____
_____
_____
_____
_____
_____
_____
_____
_____

DAY Nine

Keep a positive attitude! No matter what type of situation that you're in, always try to find the positive. For instance, when we lost our homes to foreclosure we found that losing the homes allowed us to learn to become better with our finances. Once you can see the good in a bad situation you will be able to make better decisions for yourself.

Do you think other people see you as a negative person? How often do you compliment other people? Can you go a day without thinking negative? Is your child a negative person? Do you have a positive attitude around your child? How often does your child see you see you upset?

_____
_____
_____
_____
_____
_____
_____
_____
_____
_____
_____
_____
_____
_____
_____
_____
_____
_____
_____
_____
_____
_____
_____

DAY Ten

JUST GO GREEN! Your environment is just as important as YOU are. There are so many ways you can be involved. Start by doing something small and work your way up. Get your children involved too. Try recycling, conserving water, and keeping your community clean by not littering.

Are you concerned about the environment? Would you consider recycling? What are some ways you can eliminate waste?

_____
_____
_____
_____
_____
_____
_____
_____
_____
_____
_____
_____
_____
_____
_____
_____
_____
_____
_____
_____
_____
_____
_____
_____

DAY Eleven

Start a journal. Writing down your feelings will help you heal. Your feelings are important and how you deal with your emotions affects your relationships. Holding on to anger will only build up and make you angrier. You don't want your child to internalize your pain. Keeping a journal will allow you to see your growth and motivate you to change your attitude about your life and the people in it. Just Let it Go!!

Do you find it difficult to write down your feelings? Are you ashamed of your feelings? How can you overcome your pain? What is the one thing you find difficult to let go?

_____

_____

_____

_____

_____

_____

_____

_____

_____

_____

_____

_____

_____

_____

_____

_____

_____

_____

_____

_____

_____

_____

_____

DAY Twelve

Keep your mind fit! You should exercise your mind everyday. Technology has slowed our thinking process because we allow computers and other devices to think for us. Your cell phone is the biggest culprit. How many phone numbers do you remember on your own? Probably not that many. Another way is to calculate math problems without a calculator. Not only will you be able to keep your mind active but no one will be able to rip you off!

How many phone numbers can you remember on your own? How quickly can you solve this problem without using a calculator:
18+99+1+2=?

_____
_____
_____
_____
_____
_____
_____
_____
_____
_____
_____
_____
_____
_____
_____
_____
_____
_____
_____
_____
_____
_____
_____

DAY *Thirteen*

Be more thankful. With that in mind, be thankful for the things that *are* instead of what they *are not*. Instead of complaining that your car is old, be thankful for having one. The woman with kids who have to wake up two hours earlier to catch the bus or the subway would agree. Take a look into other people's lives that do not have the things that you do.

How do you think it will affect your child if you are not thankful?
What lessons are you teaching your child about being thankful?

_____

_____

_____

_____

_____

_____

_____

_____

_____

_____

_____

_____

_____

_____

_____

_____

_____

_____

_____

_____

_____

_____

_____

DAY Fourteen

Plan a day with your friends. You probably crave for some adult interaction so why not go and hang out with some people with your same interests. That interaction may foster some new relationships that you never knew existed.

How often do you see your friends? Do you speak to your friends regularly? When was the last time you went out with some of your friends?

_____
_____
_____
_____
_____
_____
_____
_____
_____
_____
_____
_____
_____
_____
_____
_____
_____
_____
_____
_____
_____
_____
_____
_____
_____
_____
_____
_____

DAY Fifteen

REVIEW

Congratulations! You're half way to the finish line. At this point you should go back to re-read what you have written. Take a break **(BUT DON'T QUIT)** from moving forward to the second half of YOUR workbook. This is YOUR guide to becoming a Better You so if you need time to complete a section now is the time to do so. Don't cheat yourself by skipping a challenge. Your plan is to **succeed** because no one plans to fail.

_____

_____

_____

_____

_____

_____

_____

_____

_____

_____

_____

_____

_____

_____

_____

_____

_____

_____

_____

_____

_____

_____

_____

_____

_____

_____

_____

_____

DAY Sixteen

Go Meditate! By now you should have reviewed your previous responses. Take a moment to meditate on the things you have learned about your TRUE self. What are the things you would like to change about yourself? How do you think your attitude will change? Will people see a change in You? Pick the perfect quiet place where you know no one will disturb you and be one with your thoughts.

_____
_____
_____
_____
_____
_____
_____
_____
_____
_____
_____
_____
_____
_____
_____
_____
_____
_____
_____
_____
_____
_____
_____
_____
_____
_____

DAY Seventeen

You have to look in the past in order to move forward in your future. Is there a challenge you would like to revisit? Maybe you would like to spend more time on a specific challenge. Now is your chance or if you rather not, use this page to do what YOU want to do. It's your life and no one else..

_____

_____

_____

_____

_____

_____

_____

_____

_____

_____

_____

_____

_____

_____

_____

_____

_____

_____

_____

_____

_____

_____

_____

_____

_____

_____

_____

_____

DAY Eighteen

Write a letter to your child's father. Be honest. Let him know how you feel. After you're done with writing everything you've always wanted to let him know about your feelings towards him, **BURN IT, RIP IT, or THROW IT AWAY!**

What are some of the things you wanted to tell him? How did you grow from that relationship with him? Do you still want to be with him? Why or Why not?

_____
_____
_____
_____
_____
_____
_____
_____
_____
_____
_____
_____
_____
_____
_____
_____
_____
_____
_____
_____
_____
_____
_____
_____
_____

DAY Nineteen

Save your pennies! Collect all the change that you have and place them into a jar. You wouldn't believe the amount of change lying around your home and at the bottom of your purse. If you get into the habit of saving your change then it will start a new habit for less spending and more saving. Get your child involved too. Make saving money a family affair. You can teach your child the difference between Needs and Wants. Do they really NEED the latest video game or do they WANT it? Do you NEED those new pairs of shoes or do you NEED to save your money? The next time you're in a store ask yourself, 'do I need it or do I want it?'

How much money do you have saved? What are you saving for? Does your child have a savings account? Do you teach your child how to save their money?

_____
_____
_____
_____
_____
_____
_____
_____
_____
_____
_____
_____
_____
_____
_____
_____
_____
_____
_____
_____
_____

DAY Twenty

Have a conversation with a woman 10+ years older and wiser than you. They are open to sharing their experiences with you. You will gain a better perspective on your own relationships with your child's father and your child. Allow them to teach you another way to handle situations rather than continuing to make the same mistakes again.

Who do you want to speak to? How do you think her experience will help you? How do you think your life will be in 10 years? What type of relationships do you want to develop?

_____
_____
_____
_____
_____
_____
_____
_____
_____
_____
_____
_____
_____
_____
_____
_____
_____
_____
_____
_____
_____
_____
_____
_____
_____

DAY Twenty-One

Create a vision board. When you have dreams and goals to accomplish your vision board will inspire you to stay focused. Rip out pictures from the pages from those old magazines you have lying around the house so that you can post them on your board. Don't worry, your board is a representation of you and there is no right or wrong way to do it. Be realistic and post things that are attainable for you in THIS lifetime.

What is your vision for your life? How can the vision board help you?
Is your vision realistic? How do feel about creating a vision board?

_____
_____
_____
_____
_____
_____
_____
_____
_____
_____
_____
_____
_____
_____
_____
_____
_____
_____
_____
_____
_____
_____
_____
_____

DAY Twenty-Two

Reevaluate your relationships. Figure out who is *for* you and who is *against* you. It doesn't matter how long or short of time you've known a person. Often times we think people are happy for our accomplishments as we are for them. Sadly, that is not the case. Determine whether that person is contributing anything positive to your life.

What qualities do you look for in a relationship with a friend? Do
you have those same qualities? Does your child have the same kind of
friends you have?

_____
_____
_____
_____
_____
_____
_____
_____
_____
_____
_____
_____
_____
_____
_____
_____
_____
_____
_____
_____
_____

DAY Twenty-Three

Have a play date with your child and their friends...okay, maybe one friend. It's very difficult to keep up with your child as a single mom. However, if you spend time with their friends you probably can tell if your child is choosing good people to surround themselves with. You want to make sure that you KNOW who your child is hanging out with. You don't want to become that parent picking up your child from jail who had no clue that their child was up to no good.

How well do you know your child's friends? Do you like their friends?
How often do you have their friends over?

_____
_____
_____
_____
_____
_____
_____
_____
_____
_____
_____
_____
_____
_____
_____
_____
_____
_____
_____
_____
_____
_____
_____
_____

DAY Twenty-Four

Let go of your inhibitions for one day. With so much criticism single moms have to endure it's no wonder why we become self-conscious. You're told, "you can't do that," or "you shouldn't do this" because you're a mother (it's worse when you're a single mom). Of course, there are limitations but at times you should be able to have a GO FOR IT attitude. So, what's stopping you?

Is there something you would like to do but are afraid to? Why or Why not? How would it make you feel if you were not able to pursue it?

_____
_____
_____
_____
_____
_____
_____
_____
_____
_____
_____
_____
_____
_____
_____
_____
_____
_____
_____
_____
_____
_____
_____
_____

DAY Twenty-Five

Let it all go! This is your time to free your mind from whatever is bothering you.

_____
_____
_____
_____
_____
_____
_____
_____
_____
_____
_____
_____
_____
_____
_____
_____
_____
_____
_____
_____
_____
_____
_____
_____
_____
_____
_____
_____
_____
_____

DAY Twenty-Six

Surprise your child for no specific reason. When you are able to, it's good to let your child know that you're always thinking of them. Just surprise them when they least expect it. Even if money is tight, it can be the smallest gesture like writing a special note and slipping it into their backpack. Whatever you chose to do, your child will love you more for it.

How often do you surprise your child? Has your child ever surprised you? What are some ways to remind your child how much you love them?

_____

_____

_____

_____

_____

_____

_____

_____

_____

_____

_____

_____

_____

_____

_____

_____

_____

_____

_____

_____

_____

_____

_____

DAY Twenty-Seven

Consider therapy. Many single moms don't have anyone they can speak to. Often times, we don't discuss our feelings and lead our family and friends to believe that everything is GREAT when it really isn't. You may be afraid to tell someone close to you how you really feel because you're afraid of the judgment and more criticism. It doesn't have to be that way because there are different forms of therapy. One way is Group Therapy. Imagine being in a group of single moms who share the same ideas and fears as you do. Go on the internet and search which type of therapy is right for you. Also, don't get discouraged because therapy can be expensive but there are so many resources that are free. If you really want the help all you have to do is your research. When all else fails start your own group.

How do you feel about going to therapy? How can you overcome your fears? What are the things you don't like about therapy? Have you ever attended a therapy session?

DAY Twenty-Eight

Battle The War Against You! They say the most critical person in your life is YOU! No one is perfect but you don't have to keep reminding yourself that you're not perfect. It's time to RE-new your thought process. However, not everyone is prepared to change immediately. Even if you complete this entire workbook, it doesn't mean that you'll be a completely changed person. It takes time to make the necessary changes in our lives. The best part of life is that YOU have the power for YOU. Don't be concerned if your girlfriend finishes this book before you do and completely changes her life in a matter of weeks. Go at your own pace.

How often do you allow your thoughts to discourage you from doing something? Do your friends and family comments affect you? How? What are some ways you can block those thoughts?

_____
_____
_____
_____
_____
_____
_____
_____
_____
_____
_____
_____
_____
_____
_____
_____
_____
_____
_____

DAY Twenty-Nine

Dear_____

(Enter Your Name Here)

This book was written with you in mind. No matter if our experiences differ, our children are who matters. We strive to be the best moms we can be and have stumbled along the way too. We've experienced foreclosures, repossessions, and heartbreak but we are still strong women. You may feel that no one else will understand what you are going through. You no longer have to think that way anymore. We know how it feels to be alone. We've experienced times of embarrassment when there wasn't enough money to pay the power bill because your account was in the negative due to overdraft fees and your paycheck didn't cover all the bank fees. These situations probably have left you frustrated, angry, and bitter. We want to say it's okay to feel that way. But what's not okay is taking your anger out on yourself, your child and their father. It's time to break the cycle and we can not continue this movement without you. "Crazy" Baby Mamas will unite and bond together to find ways for our children to have positive male role models they desire and need in their lives. By the time you read this, we may have endured more set backs but we have learned that as long as you have a positive network of family and friends to support you then anything is possible. We will continue to encourage the men who have abandoned their duties as a Father upon us by keeping the door open for meaningful communication. We will continue to learn to forgive our children's Fathers and forget the past. Love Yourself!

Sincerely,

Max-Laine & Melanie

DAY Thirty

This is your opportunity to leave yourself a Final Note. Only you can determine your own destiny. These challenges were created for you to Become a Better YOU!

End this chapter of your life with your own ending. Write a letter to yourself. Say the things you need to hear. Leave all your worries and desires here on these pages.

_____
_____
_____
_____
_____
_____
_____
_____
_____
_____
_____
_____
_____
_____
_____
_____
_____
_____
_____
_____
_____
_____
_____
_____
_____
_____

Max-Laine is an author, screenwriter, producer, and motivational speaker. After being laid off, her future looked bleak in a struggling economy. In addition to losing her job, she lost her home to foreclosure and shortly after her car was repossessed. She did not allow this situation to deter her from pursuing her dreams of becoming a writer. Thus far, she has written three screenplays, produced short films, and co-wrote books for children. She holds a Bachelor's degree in Communications from Florida International University. She currently lives in Atlanta, Georgia with her ten-year old daughter and dog Maya.

Melanie Bent is a Senior Software Support Consultant turned author from Queens, New York. She received her Bachelor's from Florida International University and Master's in Health Law from Nova Southeastern University. She focuses on giving back to others through philanthropic activities to educate others about creating a better life for themselves and their children. In her spare time, you will find her with a camera and a pen and paper as she enjoys photography and writing poetry. She currently lives in Atlanta, Georgia with her six year old son and dog Izzy.